MINISTRY IN CRISIS

MINISTRY IN CRISIS

Changing Perspectives
on Ordination and
the Priesthood
of All Believers

ROY A.
HARRISVILLE

AUGSBURG Publishing House • Minneapolis

MINISTRY IN CRISIS
Changing Perspectives on Ordination and the Priesthood of All Believers

Scripture quotations, unless otherwise noted, are from the Revised Standard Version of the Bible, copyright 1946, 1952, and 1971 by the Division of Christian Education of the National Council of Churches.

Library of Congress Cataloging-in-Publication Data

Harrisville, Roy A.
  MINISTRY IN CRISIS.

  Bibliography: p.
  1. Pastoral theology.   I. Title.
BV4011.H336   1987   262'.1   87-19548
ISBN 0-8066-2318-7

Manufactured in the U.S.A.   APH 10-4441

1   2   3   4   5   6   7   8   9   0   1   2   3   4   5   6   7   8   9

*To Alvin N. Rogness,
predecessor, superior, and friend*

Contents

Preface

This little volume contains the C. C. Hein Lectures, delivered in April 1987 at Pacific Lutheran Theological Seminary in Berkeley, California; Trinity Lutheran Seminary in Columbus, Ohio; Wartburg Theological Seminary in Dubuque, Iowa; and at my own school, Luther Northwestern Theological Seminary in St. Paul, Minnesota.

Thanks are due the Presiding Bishop of The American Lutheran Church, Dr. David Preus, the Executive Secretary of its Division for Theological Education and Ministry, Dr. Walter Wietzke, and the presidents of the seminaries named, for their gracious invitation to me to appear as Hein Lecturer this year.

Anyone who has worked in the Christian community as pastor or teacher has spent time reflecting on the public ministry, its dilemmas or its significance. Few, however, have had time or opportunity to give to that reflection any proper order or shape. I have not been among those few, for which reason I am grateful for the stimulus to more careful study furnished by the invitation to deliver these lectures. I am grateful also to the faculties, students, and pastors present at the various institutions for kindnesses shown me while on their campuses and for patient attention to my argument.

Some of my oldest friends will be in considerable disagreement with what I state here. To them I can only respond that, despite whatever prejudice or errors in fact and interpretation they believe they may detect, I am presuming on their friendship to hear me out.

1

The Crisis

Diagnosis and Treatment

The Crisis

When we hear the word *crisis,* we often think of someone sick with a raging fever. The fever may "break" and the patient recover, or the disease may kill or maim the patient for life. The situation is "critical"—things may go either way. Those who pay attention to "ministry" in the Christian community frequently state that it is in critical condition. Things may go either way. But what is not always clear is what is meant by that evaluation. To what, for example, does *ministry* in that diagnosis refer? In the New Testament, the word most often translated "ministry" is a nonbiblical, nonreligious term applied to a great variety of functions which are totally free of associations with title or position. Still, the concentration appears to be upon what is called "the office of the ministry," or the "ordained ministry," though that term *ordained* tends to compound the confusion. The accent, then, is on persons who earn their keep with standing in more or less confined spaces in houses of worship, addressing congregations willing to keep to their seats and listen. And as for *crisis*, what is not clear is whether that condition is something which affects persons who engage in this peculiar activity from the outside, somehow analogous to a virus; whether the condition is self-induced, as in a crisis of self-consciousness; or whether it is a combination of the two, since the one can easily furnish the impulse for the other. Or is that condition something which does not affect those persons so much as what they do, whether from the outside, inside, or an alternation of both?

Symptom and Treatment

Rather than beginning with picking the diagnosis apart, it might be more useful to note the symptom alleged to indicate the crisis. From what I read, the symptom of the crisis consists in an imbalance—primarily, an imbalance in the minister's self-understanding or the minister's activity and its perception by those who witness it or are the objects of it. This problem of the relation between the "office of the ministry" and the "universal priesthood of all believers" is as old as Methuselah, but it is the inability to determine in what that relation consists which is said to constitute the imbalance.

As far as I am able to tell, those who are after treating the symptom, if not the crisis itself, are divided principally into two camps. The one asserts that salvation is provided through the ministerial office. When the clergy is conscious of itself in analogy to Jesus Christ, that is, when it is conscious that it is constitutive of life with God here or hereafter, the imbalance should begin to disappear. This is an idea most often associated with Roman Catholic teaching, but there are Lutherans who entertain it. One writes that the minister has the "keys" to the kingdom of heaven. The pastor alone has the authority to "loose," to forgive the penitent, and the authority to "bind," to shut heaven against the obdurate. Absolution is thus the most official and characteristic pronouncement of the minister. Those words in the "Brief Order for Confession and Forgiveness" in the *Lutheran Book of Worship*—

> as a called and ordained minister of the Church of Christ, and by his authority, I therefore declare to you the entire forgiveness of all your sins[1]—

do not appear to be at such great remove from that view, considering the subject of the sentence. But if this group draws some sort of "ontological" distinction between the preacher and the pew, another regards the distinction between them as merely functional.

According to this second view, the minister does what all baptized Christians are authorized to do, but which they assign to a single person for the sake of order. All believers have the right to baptize, to preach, teach, and absolve, but delegate these responsibilities to individuals they select so as to inhibit confusion in the church. When the clergy is conscious of itself in analogy to an officeholder in a republic, so the argument reads, the imbalance should begin to disappear.

Corollary in Views of Ordination

The corollary of this divided opinion respecting the symptom of imbalance is the divided opinion regarding the nature of that event which is alleged to make the minister a minister: ordination. For the group which draws an "ontological" distinction between the ministerial office and the universal priesthood, a special grace is given the ordinand through the "laying on of hands"—something of essence or power, equipping and empowering for the office of ministry. When one Lutheran writes that ordination does not merely consist in a commission but "in the gift of a new being, or of a new being in a new relation,"[2] I take him to mean that ordination has something to do with the conferring of essence or substance. That ordination prayer in our *Occasional Services*[3]—

> Eternal God, through your Son, Jesus Christ, pour out your Holy Spirit upon __name__ and fill *him/her* with the gifts of grace [for the ministry of Word and Sacrament]—

may not be so far from that view. And if the pastor alone has the "power of the keys," and if that power is conferred in ordination, then a redemptive significance attaches to ordination, since only the ordained can shut or open heaven. On the other hand, for that group which regards the distinction between pastor and people as functional, the event of ordination merely corroborates the people's choice; it is the transference of office by the universal priesthood to one of its members, and is without redemptive significance.

This division of opinion has also had a long history, punctuated with the names of our theological ancestors, of our forebears and the founders of our "synods" in this country. Among the Germans in New York or Iowa and Missouri, Johannes Grabau and C. F. W. Walther rushed at each other full tilt over "office," "universal priesthood," and ordination. Among Scandinavians, pastors of the Norwegian Evangelical Lutheran Church in America labeled their counterparts in the Eielsen or Hauge synods "papirpresten" (paper pastors)—mere licensees.

Inefficiency of the Treatment

Is there hope that the one or other treatment of the imbalance will ultimately heal the crisis? Will summoning the patient to recognize the essential difference between the office and the universal priesthood check the symptom? It has often been said by those who urge the difference that, of course, a distinction must be made between the person who holds the office and that office itself.

The preacher demands respect, not for the sake of the person, but of the office. That is a rather fine distinction, but if observation means anything, or if the past teaches anything, the distinction is theoretical, scarcely held to in the concrete. For when has a preacher not erased the distinction with identifying some personal cause, some private project with the will of God? The end of such things is keeping the universal priesthood under tutelage. Substituting the power of rule for that imbalance in self-understanding may eliminate the symptom only to bring on another, new disease. The preacher-tyrant, fired with the consciousness of incarnating the ideal, with the awareness of an essential difference between "them" and "us," is not well, though perhaps happy. Socrates would dispute even that. Of the soul goaded by the "sting of desire," the old Athenian said that "it must always be poverty-stricken, unsatisfied, and haunted by fear."

> Now when Jesus was born in Bethlehem of Judea in the days of Herod the king, behold, wise men from the East came to Jerusalem saying, "Where is he who has been born king of the Jews? For we have seen his star in the East, and have come to worship him." When Herod the king heard this, he was troubled, and all Jerusalem with him. . . .
>
> (Matt. 2:1-3).

Or will the symptom be checked with summoning the patient to acknowledge that what he does, what she does, all have the right to do but merely delegate for the sake of order? At present, a considerable number of congregations function in analogy to the republic. In traditionally democratic fashion, they require men and women prepared for ministry to "campaign" for it—subject to nominations, interviews (including those with spouse), candidating, and election. The old "trial sermon," once scorned as verging on blasphemy by those who accented the difference in essence, has become commonplace. Where travel is not convenient, some "call committees" now request televised sermons from their nominees. Is the Christian community a republic, a democracy with "all power to the people"? In 1523, Martin Luther wrote that a Christian assembly or community had the right and power to judge all doctrine; to call, install, or depose all ministers or teachers, and derived that right from Scripture. It is false to assume, however, that for Luther the doctrine of the universal priesthood constituted a "democratic" principle or the application of the idea of popular sovereignty to the church. That doctrine was the consequence of the gospel, spoken to all, thus entrusted to all—the only treasure of the church—and for which all are responsible.

Most congregations till now seem to possess an infinite patience, willing to endure a great deal from those who fill their pulpits (provided they do not regard the laxity of the clergy as occurring to their own advantage, a benediction on their own negligence). But, with shrinkage in membership, missions, and funds, who can predict whether or not

the minister of tomorrow will be as anxious an occupant of the pulpit as those whom the citizenry
with one exception has budged from its oval office,
whether by assassination, impeachment, or non-
election following a single term, and for almost 30
years?

> And he came to Nazareth . . . and he went to the
> synagogue. . . . And he said to them . . . "there
> were many widows in Israel in the days of Elijah
> . . . and Elijah was sent to none of them but only
> to Zarephath . . . to a woman who was a widow."
> . . . And they rose up and put him out of the city,
> and led him to the brow of the hill on which their
> city was built, that they might throw him down
> headlong. . . .
>
> (Luke 4:16-29)

The Camp of "Both-And"

Naturally, between these two camps there hud-
dles a third, the camp of "both-and." "Both-and"
will check the symptom, that absence of equilibri-
um. *Both* the office *and* the universal priesthood are
necessary. Neither can abolish or minimize the
need for the other. The office of ministry is *both* a
gift for service *and* a delegation of service. The universal priesthood *both* includes preparation for the
office of ministry *and* excludes arrogating to oneself
the occupancy of that office willy-nilly. "Both-and"
frees the one from competition with the other;
"both-and" regards neither as supplementing the
other; "both-and" enables holding firm to one and

the other. But "both-and" will no more check the symptom than will construing the office of ministry after the analogy of Christ or of the local elected official. And the reason is that all three responses to the symptom are oriented to the question of *power*, of right or authority, its "checks and balances."

2

"Once Upon a Time"

Charism and Office in the New Testament

The Variety of Offices

"Once upon a time" lived the community which produced our New Testament. In that community there was an incredible variety of "offices." If we have managed to collapse that original multiplicity into the single "office" of preaching the gospel and administering the sacraments, there is nothing in the life of that community to justify it. To his enthusiasts at Corinth their founder wrote:

> To one is given . . . the utterance of wisdom, and to another the utterance of knowledge, . . . to another faith, . . . to another gifts of healing, . . . to

another the working of miracles, to another prophecy, to another the ability to distinguish between
spirits, to another various kinds of tongues, to another the interpretation of tongues.

(1 Cor. 12:8-10)

Again:

God has appointed in the church first apostles, second prophets, third teachers, then workers of miracles, then healers, helpers, administrators, speak-
ers in various kinds of tongues.

(1 Cor. 12:28)

Or again:

Having gifts that differ according to the grace given
to us, let us use them: if prophecy, in proportion to
our faith; if service, in our serving; he who teaches,
in his teaching; he who exhorts, in his exhortation;
he who contributes, in liberality; he who gives aid,
with zeal; he who does acts of mercy, with cheer-
fulness.

(Rom. 12:6-8)

These lists are hardly an encouragement to Christians to broaden their definition of the ministerial
office, as though Corinth, for example, were divided into givers and takers, leaders and led, the one
allowing the other merely to join in the Collect for
the day. The situation at Corinth was quite the re-
verse—how to harness such an explosion of offices
so as to serve a common purpose? And as for the

designations of those offices, with the exception of the term "apostle" or the phrase "the Twelve," not a single one originated with the new faith. All had long been current in paganism or Judaism. Those earliest congregations apparently cared little whether or not the general public confused their prophets with, say, Stoic preachers. The variety, the explosion demanded improvisation, an expropriation of names, titles, and positions from anywhere at all to designate the activity.

No Golden Age

This does not mean that "once upon a time" there was a great golden age in which all was balance and harmony. Thanks to the researches of the great 19th-century scholar, Ferdinand Christian Baur, we have been disabused of the romantic notion that the primitive Christian community was one single, Arthur S. Sullivan chord "from the soul of the organ." There was crisis aplenty, and accompanying symptoms enough to drive an apostle to despair:

> Each one of you says, "I belong to Paul," or "I belong to Apollos," or "I belong to Cephas," or "I belong to Christ." Is Christ divided? Was Paul crucified for you?
>
> (1 Cor. 1:12-13)

Not even the apostles, those towering and self-contained figures, holding unrepeatable office, and later restricted to the circle of "the Twelve," were free of challenge—from others or even from each other.

That line—"when Cephas came to Antioch I opposed him to his face"—was written by an apostle,
and in language used to expose a heretic or a quack.
There was no golden age. "Once upon a time" the
same symptom existed as exists now, signaling the
same crisis as exists now, but the criticism of that
symptom was radically different from our own.
That criticism was different because it refused to
treat at the level of power, however the principals
in those earliest struggles may have interpreted
their differences. The Jesus whose sayings and
doings the earliest community had husbanded and
transmitted had called to abandon all claim to power:

> You know that those who are supposed to rule over
> the Gentiles lord it over them, and their great men
> exercise authority over them. But it shall not be so
> among you; but whoever would be great among you
> must be your servant, and whoever would be first
> among you must be slave of all.
>
> (Mark 10:42-44)

And when the Jesus of Matthew says that "all who
take the sword will perish by the sword" (Matt.
26:52), I take that to mean that desire for power
does not end in its possession, but in the loss of
power.

What furnished the stimulus for preserving such
tradition was the recognition that power was nothing but another name for God, for the God who in
Jesus was repossessing the world he had made, and

in that conquest was crushing to death whatever human beings had established to secure themselves or their identity. It was the recognition that before this God one could only be a subject, never a ruler; an occupant, a lessee, never an owner; a taker and never a giver, and that the witness to this conquering and shattering was not to remain idea or theory, but to be made concrete in how those who stood before such a deity stood with one another. This recognition rendered the criticism of that symptom of imbalance so radically different from our own—"once upon a time."

Charism and Office in Paul

Nowhere in the documents of that earliest community is this criticism brought to sharper focus than in the writings of the one most proximate to the event that signaled that conquest of God, but, for all that, the one least understood and hence least authoritative in the generations after him—Paul of Tarsus. *Charisma* was the concept he used by which to check the imbalance. *Charisma*, "gift," as opposed to the "pneumatic" or "spiritual"—terms with their home in the old Hellenistic notions of power, person, and class. And since God's repossession of the world in Jesus Christ was not merely judgment but also promise, all who bracketed "power" with "God" had become takers in fact, not merely in theory. All had become "charismatics." But if all were charismatics, then no distinction could be drawn between activities once restricted to the religious and others relegated to the secular or profane. "And God has appointed . . . healers, helpers, administrators." And, if all were charismatics, then even what had once been regarded as inherited or derived from nature was now labeled "gift," since everything which belonged to the existence of those who acknowledged that before the Giver they could only be takers was made to share his life:

> For us there is one God, the Father, from whom are all things and for whom we exist, and one Lord, Jesus Christ, through whom are all things and through whom we exist.
>
> (1 Cor. 8:6)

Facticity, then, the mere occurrence of an activity (in modern parlance, the mere filling of an "office") spelled nothing—least of all genuineness. How could it when all held "office"? The test of a charism lay in its use, use for the other. But if use for the other was all, then charism was not only gift, but also ordeal. Grace had made alive, but also burned up its taker. Of the messenger whom his Philippians suspected of malingering, Paul wrote:

> Receive him . . . he nearly died for the work of Christ, risking his life to complete your service to me.
>
> (Phil. 2:29-30)

If it was true that God was winning back the world he had made, and that those who came to believe it were made to share God's life, then the shape of their existence had already been determined, and by the event through which God had begun his conquest and given his life to share—in Jesus, the crucified. Then "charism" was nothing but Paul's projection of justification into ecclesiology:

> God gives life to the dead and, through the invasion of grace, sets up his kingdom where before demons and demonic energies held sway. . . . God creates among the rebels that *pax Christi,* which is at once the subjection, the reconciliation and the new creation of the cosmos. Godless men become obedient and are endowed with charismatic gifts; this is the eschatological miracle, the decisive action of God in his divine majesty, the triumph of grace over the world of wrath.[4]

For, if because of Christ's death the godless through faith were given to share God's life—and this is what justification by faith means—then life could only be what it is for God: life for the other. Then use was all.

To the degree Paul's criticisms held, to that degree the structure of his churches was loose. Old Testament distinctions of rank, title, or position were absent. There was no council of elders appointed according to age or seniority, as may have been the case in Palestinian congregations. Who preached at Thessalonica, Galatia, or Rome? Who presided at the Supper in Corinth? There is not a single word in Paul respecting that aristocratic form of government which one professor (Leonhard Hütter), 50 years after Luther at Wittenberg, had suggested was best for the church.

Now, the structures of those churches may have been loose, but they were not anarchic. Paul was not an advocate of organizational chaos. The church at Philippi had bishops and deacons (Phil. 1:1), and to the ecstasy and loss of control at Corinth, the greatest charismatic of them all (and scarcely to his own advantage!) opposed reason and order:

> How can any one in the position of an outsider say the "Amen" to your thanksgiving when he does not know what you are saying? . . . If any speak in a tongue, let there be only two or at most three, and each in turn; and let one interpret. . . . If a revelation is made to another sitting by, let the first be silent.
> (1 Cor. 14:16,27,30)

At the worship, it appeared, the Spirit could be ordered to sit down.

The Sohm/Harnack Controversy

This state of affairs did not last. Some 70 years ago, two great historians pommeled each other in books, monographs, articles, and essays over the reason why. The one, Rudolf Sohm, asserted that earliest Christianity was anarchistic in structure; that activities in the church resulted from immediate inspiration. This "charismatic organization," wrote Sohm, was free of and contradicted all juridical or legal order. Naturally, with the growth of the assemblies, persons had to be chosen to preach or preside at the Supper, but the choice itself was a revelation of the divine will; it too occurred by way of inspiration. So the charism did not exclude the choice, and the choice was not to an office or function apart from the charism—both came through immediate inspiration. The heretics, Sohm argued, retained the church's original structure, since their leaders held no titles by virtue of law, but emerged on the spur, from moment to moment. And it was precisely from this charismatic anarchy, Sohm contended, that the church as a legal, juridical structure evolved. It did so because of the earliest community's naive identification of the people of God with an external, visible fellowship. By neglecting to distinguish between the people of God as visible only to faith, and the people of God as external fellowship, earliest Christianity prepared for Catholicism. On the last page of his monograph on the essence and origin of Catholicism, Sohm wrote:

In Catholicism, the essence of the Christian community in the religious sense (the ecclesia), and thus the essence of Christianity, is given legal, formal character. Humanity's life with God is bound to specific ecclesiastical forms. The "divine," legal system of the church is determinative for religious life, since the church of ecclesiastical law is the church in the religious sense. . . . Because primitive Christianity possessed merely the religious concept of the church, and as a result applied this concept to the external, visible Christian community as well, with the rise of legal system as applied to the Christian community (the church in the religious sense), Catholicism of necessity emerged from primitive Christianity.[5]

Adolf von Harnack was of another opinion. From the very beginning, he argued, the structure of the church was twofold—charismatic, worldwide *and* legal, local. Proclamation of the word rested on the charism of the apostle, the prophet, or teacher, the organization of the church conceived as from God. But the arrangement of the local congregation rested on the election of officers of an "administrative type," after the fashion of the Roman state. In the local organization, Harnack argued, the charismatic began to retreat before the legal—the activity of apostle, prophet, or teacher was transferred to those officers of "administrative type." Thus for Harnack, the legal organization, not the charismatic, as Sohm had supposed, provided stimulus for the further development of the church, a development which resulted in the monarchical episcopate, first as an office within the congregation, then as an office within the total church. The monarchical bishop was merely the exponent of the individual congregation, self-contained and sovereign. Harnack wrote:

"The divine ecclesiastical law" was present from the beginning, though it did not yet have the scope and setting which it later received. . . . Since, in assessing the church, its visibility was taken up into its essence, the eucharistic assembly was held to be the most important form of visibility. But such an assembly is inconceivable without order. Order required leaders, and the status of the leaders had to be fixed. Thus arose the idea of the leaders as irremoveable by virtue of divine right. This gave birth to Catholicism as well as to ecclesiastical law, since a certain number of individuals singled out by God through the charism now obtained the rank of officials with a legal claim to obedience. . . . This gave rise to ecclesiastical law . . . as a divine, i.e., Catholic, ecclesiastical law. For, so it was taught, officials were officials by virtue of divine decree and, as such, indispensable to the community.[6]

Which reason to choose—"Sohm or Rome"? Neither reason is correct. Both assume a contest between the charismatic and the "administrative" in earliest Christianity, because both begin where Sohm accused Harnack of beginning—with a modern concept of the church as juridical structure distinct from the state, but still belonging within the sphere of the state. The only difference between them is that Sohm deplored that Enlightenment doctrine, whereas Harnack appeared to affirm it.

The New Testament community did not regard charism and office as the final realities. It did not construe them as competitors—the struggle in Acts to embrace them in dialectic, however tenuous, is evidence enough of that. Nowhere in the New Testament does there appear a chaotic freedom of the Spirit or of individual persons filled with the Spirit. Happily, we are past the point of ultra-Protestant

anxiety at discovering aspects of order in primitive
Christianity. But for Paul, at least, *modality,* not the
facticity of the charism, was decisive, and authority
was acknowledged in the concretely occurring service. And, nowhere in the New Testament is order
proclaimed as holy law. Nowhere is the church conceived as a museum for patriarchal behavior or an
arena for the advocacy of human rights. Nowhere
in the New Testament is the apostolate viewed as
transferable institution, and nowhere do the
"keys," does absolution take on significance for
clerical self-consciousness. Neither the authoritar-
ian, "Catholic" nor the liberal, "Protestant" concept
of the church reflects the actual conditions in primitive Christianity. What was decisive was the link
between Spirit and the word, the "tradition," the
witness to what God had begun in Jesus. These
were the ultimate realities, and made an absolutiz-
ing of Spirit over against the tradition, or an ab-
solutizing of the tradition over against the Spirit
impossible. With all its diversity, what held the
church together was its witness to the Christ. The
New Testament thus yields no evidence of what
scholars for years have labeled "early Catholicism."

Evidence of Anxiety

The New Testament, however, does give evidence of anxiety, anxiety for the tradition, for its
drying up, and with that anxiety there occurs a
subtle shift, a barely perceptible tacking to the
wind—and in the direction of appointments or order or offices or structures as had existed in the

past, whether at Palestine or Rome. And that shift, however slight, had its birth in still another, in an alteration of faith from the acknowledgment that in Jesus Christ God was making conquest, that the sign of that conquest was life or use for the other in those who were his, to the assumption that the conquest somehow needed guaranteeing, that the worldwide body of Christ was in reality a house of God that needed protecting. There is some difference between these lines:

> Being found in human form *he* humbled *himself* and became obedient. . . . Therefore God has highly exalted *him* and bestowed on *him* the name which is above every name, that *at the name of Jesus* every knee should bow, in heaven and on earth and under the earth, and every tongue confess that *Jesus Christ* is Lord, to the glory of God the Father . . .
>
> (Phil. 2:8-11)

and these lines:

> [God] raised *us* up with him, and made *us* sit with him in the heavenly places in Christ Jesus. . . .
>
> (Eph. 2:6)

The difference is that what once was said of God could now be said of the "house of God." And if that house should need regulating or protecting, then the attitude toward "outsiders" could alter, from this:

> I could wish that I myself were accursed and cut off from Christ for the sake of my brethren
>
> (Rom. 9:1)

perhaps to this:

> Those who afflict you . . . shall suffer the punish-
> ment of eternal destruction and exclusion from the
> presence of the Lord and from the glory of his
> might.
>
> (2 Thess. 1:6ff.)

And once the authority for that protection was attached to individuals, the notion of ecclesiastical
office would need only time for its gestation.

On that shift, and sprung from that alteration in
faith—barely perceptible in the New Testament, but
for all that still perceptible—the majority of the
churches in Christianity have struggled to establish
existence for two thousand years. That shift would
some day come to be regarded as the essence of
the matter, and the time of its occurring as the
"golden age" to which every attempt at reform or
rejuvenation should return.

It may be an advantage that we humans have an
instinct for forgetting what was dismal in our past
and reminding ourselves only of what was good in
it and gilding it, dubbing it "golden." But that instinct is also a disadvantage, since we are also historical beings and the law of history is change, and
that longing for the golden past works against our
capacity for change. When present existence is op-
pressive, when crisis occurs, remembrance and cus-
tom fire that instinct in us against moving into a
future that is unknown and may be dreadful. That
instinct for survival through return becomes even

stronger when crisis raises in us the suspicion that history is no longer the horizon of God's conquest but the reality itself. The perspective from which the great interpreter of Jesus sought to restore sanity to his churches has never been that of mainline Christianity—only of the sects. Is it true, then, as has been argued, that the apostle Paul, who all his life struggled against fanaticism, could not establish churchly tradition, but could only depose it, because he overtaxed the Christian and the fellowship of the church, and thus could only give stimulus to fanaticism again?[7] Is it true that the notion of charism as given to all, since all had been given God's life to share, and that *for this reason* use for the other was all, just as it was for God; that *on this account* love, that human impossibility become possible through faith, was the only court of appeal; that *because of this* whatever authority existed consisted only in the concretely occurring service—is it true that such a perspective was greater than the church's capacity for change, and that this explains the isolation of the apostle to the Gentiles and his gospel? Is this the reason why, as some have said, the Christian "left" is unable to cut itself adrift from hypotheses of an age dead and gone, its link to the developments of modern science no more intimate than that of a Stalin to an Einstein, its call to "liberation" often a liturgical-magical formula for escape? Can the imbalance be checked or the crisis passed with the acknowledgment of God's repossession of the world in the crucified, or is that eschatological view more than a church can manage?

Is the anxiety in face of such a sovereignty greater than the taste for the freedom it promises?

To put the question in another form, is the symptom to which we have been referring actually the symptom, or is it the crisis? Is the crisis in ministry precisely the refusal to allow for a lack of balance, or whatever passes for balance with us, because balance, parity, equivalence all have their origin in what God rejected as the instruments for his conquest?

> But God chose what is weak in the world to shame the strong, God chose what is low and despised in the world, even things that are not, to bring to nothing things that are. . . .
>
> (1 Cor. 1:27-28)

3

The Resistible Rise of the Hierarchy

A Historical Sketch

The Thread from the Tangled Knot

Since I will attempt something of a historical sketch in this chapter, a few remarks respecting history and the writing of it may be in order. One European author of historical essays avers that history is simply a branch of literature; that the mass of what has actually occurred—whether in a single day or over the millennia—will remain forever unknown and unknowable. Whatever emerges from that mass as "history" is merely something determined by the historian, who pulls at a thread from that tangled knot and weaves an intellectual "novel" from it.[8] In less genteel fashion, Voltaire once said that history is "only a pack of tricks we play on the dead." The judgment is a bit extreme, but may be more accurate than the assumption that some sure-fire method exists which can guarantee access to historical reality. The concession that we can know reality only in a limited way, that it is impossible for us to distill final causes from historical occurrence, or, Christianly speaking, that we cannot know what only God can know, and for this reason need not attempt it or despair at being incapable of it is a healthy perspective from which to do historical work. Naturally, this concession does not free us of responsibility for seeing as clearly as we can what we are able to see. The great Swabian biblical interpreter Adolf Schlatter once described the historian's task as seeing and seeing and more seeing. But the knowledge of our limits may free us to see whatever it is we are able to see.

The thread I've pulled from the tangled knot of earliest Christian history, and with which I'm after weaving my own "novel," is God's repossession of the world in Jesus Christ, which when embraced by faith gives a share in the life of God, and is signaled in existence for the other. Some, many, but not all have tugged at that thread. It is not acknowledged by all that primitive Christianity was fired with the eschatological vision of God's having begun to draw all things to himself in the death of Jesus of Nazareth, and that from such a vision derived everything it thought, said, and did. Nor is it acknowledged by all that, however proximate he may have been to the event of Jesus of Nazareth, Paul of Tarsus must be regarded as its chief interpreter. Many still regard him as at great distance from Jesus, as the "second founder" of Christianity, perhaps even as the perverter of the gospel of Jesus. This is not how I see it, and my purpose has been to persuade you to see what I see, or at least persuade you to postpone your adverting to my blindness till I tell you what I see.

On occasion, I ask my students if the names of colleagues now dead, but who left something behind in print, mean anything to them. The response is depressingly minimal, but scarcely surprising. This was not true of Paul. A wave of oblivion did not pass over him the day he died. It is true, among those second-century Christians whom we call the "apostolic fathers," or among the earliest apologists, Paul is scarcely cited by name. But those worthies were not ignorant of Paul, as the quantity of their allusions or the coincidence in language indicates. What is significant is what they retained from Paul—in sum, a Paul reduced, bent, warped, tailored to their notion of "orthodoxy" or whatever passed for it. What was the reason for trimming Paul to size?

The "Rehabilitation" of Paul and the Parousia's Delay

Part of the answer is that Paul was the Bible of the enemy. That enemy believed that between this world and God there was an unbridgeable gap; that the self, the "I," spirit or soul was unalterably divine, but had been imprisoned and benumbed by the world; that only a "call" from the world of light could free it, and that at the end what was divine in the human would return to its true home. The list of heretics who found their "vision" already there in Paul (and vision it was—something experienced in a trice, not arrived at through scientific study or education) is a list as long as your arm: Simon Magus, the Ophites (snake people), Basilides, Marcion, Valentinus, Ptolemy, Theodotus. Paul's reference to what had been "hidden" from "the rulers of this age" (1 Cor. 2:7-8) and from human thought had its analogy in the enemy's "vision" as an esoteric possession, unrecognizable to the evil powers of the world. Like Paul, the enemy too could boast that through his "vision" he had been liberated from all external authority, that "all things" were "lawful" (cf. 1 Cor. 6:12; 10:23), but like Paul could also add that not only knowledge of the self, but also steadfastness in the path of that knowledge was decisive. And throbbing at the center of the enemy's "vision" lay expectation, an "eschatological" hope. Paul's words concerning "the appointed time" as having "grown very short," of the shape of "this world" as "passing away" (1 Cor. 7:29,31), have their counterpart in these lines from a second-century Gnostic fragment:

> The times are cut short and the days have shortened and our time has been fulfilled, and the weeping of our destruction has approached us.[9]

But if the enemy's doctrine of salvation reflected a notion of the "unworldly self" at odds with nature and creation, it also embraced a fellowship which distanced itself from the this-sided fraternities of antiquity. The enemy drew his adherents from the plebs and from women, in contrast to the remainder of society which cared little for the plight of the oppressed and exploited. Both Paul and the enemy inclined to a "charismatic" understanding of the fellowship. For both, the "congregation" was to rule over its own occasions, establish its own functionaries, and care for its own feasts. "Not all things are helpful" (1 Cor. 6:12); "not all things build up" (1 Cor. 10:23) could as easily have been uttered by a Gnostic as by Paul. For both, use was all.

If Paul was the Bible of the heretic, the church had still another "enemy"— the Lord himself who had delayed his coming, and with that delay threw in doubt the assertion that at the cross God had vindicated his Messiah, exalted him as Son of man and Lord, and had begun conquest. The delay called for adjustment, adjustment to time and to visibility. If Paul's rehabilitation is already reflected in our New Testament, so is Christ's. Let these words from 2 Peter, which have more the aspect of a complaint than a comfort, stand in evidence:

> Do not ignore this one fact, beloved, that with the Lord one day is as a thousand years, and a thousand years as one day.
>
> (2 Peter 3:8)

The fire of expectation had been banked; the conviction that the time was short, that the Christians' sufferings were merely flaws attaching to an interim, had gone begging. At any rate, in one way or another, for one reason or another, what Paul had preached was muted. "Sitting it out" demanded order.

The Route to Hierarchy

And the route to order was the hierarchy. "Let the flock of Christ have peace with the presbyters set over it," wrote Clement of Rome.[10] "I cried out while I was with you, I spoke with a great voice,—with God's own voice—'Give heed to the bishop, and to the presbytery and deacons,' " wrote Ignatius of Antioch.[11] To guarantee that the pure doctrine had been transmitted without a break, Hegesippus of Asia Minor constructed a list of bishops reaching back to the apostles. For Clement of Alexandria, the teacher, the Christian "Gnostic" was "after the image and likeness of God," the "organ of the divine voice," a "living image" of the Lord.[12] In Rome, Hippolytus asserted that bishops received the Spirit as successors of the apostles, that in their consecration grace had taken on official, peculiar, differentiated shape. With Cyprian of Carthage the hierarchy attained to its full height—the bishop and he alone could speak the word of judgment or salvation. What remained was to extend the bishop's authority for excommunication to an authority over every aspect of the church's life—with the sixth canon of Nicea and its decree that none could be bishop without the consent of the Metropolitans of Alexandria, Antioch, or Rome; with the Synod of Sardica and the resultant appointment of the Roman bishop as umpire of the Christian world; with the assertion of Leo I that since Peter (equipped by Christ with the fullness of his power and set over the other apostles) continued his activity in his successors, the bishop of Rome was the *vicarius Christi*, entrusted with care for the whole church, and, finally, with the decree of Pope Gelasius that both temporal and spiritual power belonged to the church. The activity of the charismatic had been transferred to the possessor of permanent office.

The reader may be aware of the theater piece by Bertolt Brecht after which this lecture is named. It is called "The Resistible Rise of Arturo Ui," an attempt to explain to capitalists Hitler's rise to power by setting it in a context they cannot miss—Alfonse Capone's Chicago. In an afterword to that piece, Brecht writes that everyday logic should not be frightened off when it deals with the centuries; that what applies in small things should also apply in large. Though people in power may allow a petty scoundrel to assume giant proportions, he does not deserve that status in our study of history. Everyday logic suggests that the rise of the hierarchy was not inevitable, but evitable; not irresistible, but resistible. The debate between those who detect an "early Catholicism" in the later New Testament writings and those who insist that such a notion blurs the division between those writings and the literature of a later century may thus be wide of the

mark. In the New Testament, neither the rehabilitation of Paul nor the occasions for it led irresistibly
to hierarchy in the church, or to a spiritual succession from one generation to another through consecration or the laying on of hands.

The Question of Resistibility

First, as to rank, it is often said that in Acts Luke
was anxious to fuse the Pauline, charismatic gospel
with the Palestinian tradition of an office of gov-
erning elders, this, then, a first step toward the
notion of succession. For this reason, the argument
proceeds, Luke records those Hellenists who baptized on their own initiative in Judea and Samaria
as having to wait for Peter's inspection trip, on
which occasion the new converts received the Spirit. "For," Luke writes, "it had not yet fallen on any
of them, but they had only been baptized in the
name of the Lord Jesus" (Acts 8:16). In Acts 10, the
situation is reversed—Cornelius and the Gentiles
believe, receive the Spirit, but undergo baptism
only at Peter's command. In either instance, the
presence of Peter is required. In the one, there is
no reception of the Spirit without him; in the other,
there is no baptism, no incorporation into the fellowship without him.

But if for Luke only the continuity of the apostolic
church can guarantee salvation (and by "church"
read the Jerusalem caliphate with Peter at its head),
that idea is imperfectly executed. Where was the
"bishop" when the eunuch was baptized (Acts

8:38)? When Luke records that an angel of the Lord chose the road on which Philip was to hitchhike, and that the Spirit of the Lord singled out the precise vehicle Philip was to flag down, the conclusion can scarcely be that the eunuch's baptism was "simply water and no baptism." What would everyday logic infer from such a narrative? Set in midst of a book alleged to reduce the Hellenists and Paul to the status of minions of the apostles (a title which Luke almost never assigns to Paul), is this story merely an erratic on the geological terrain, an exception to prove the rule that position in life is everything, or could it be Luke's tongue in cheek to everything written before or after—the admission that when all is said and done, the Spirit is sovereign over rank; that, in the language of another New Testament author hostile to hierarchy, the Spirit "blows where it wills" (John 3:8)?

Second, as to succession, it is often alleged that with the Pastorals the church is "on a roll" toward the monarchical episcopate—and all of it in Paul's own backyard. The allegation may be correct. The concept of charisma as given to all appears to retreat before the notion of charisma as conveyed through consecration. But everyday logic inquires, Why was that "roll" aborted? Why did the manufacture of the Pastorals—if manufacture it was—which obviously did not balk at rehabilitating Paul almost to the point of anonymity, or showed no anxiety in face of setting the letters to Titus and Timothy within any conceivable chronology of Paul's life, why did it stop short of apostolic succession? Reference to the Spirit in the Pastorals is slight; slighter still the references to the Spirit in the Christian. But immediately following the author's reminder of the charism given his pupil at ordination, he writes "for God did not give us a Spirit of cowardice but of power and love and sobriety" (2 Tim. 1:7, my translation). Here, at least, the Pastorals have fallen in with Paul. It was "sobriety," a concept extracted from popular philosophy and pressed into the service of love, of use for the other, by which Paul had demolished all distinctions (cf. Rom. 12:3). Could that little verse be to the Pastorals what the story of the eunuch is to Acts?

The Concept of Petrine Succession

We need to pause for a moment before returning to the question of resistibility. In current study of the literature following the New Testament period, there is a tendency to assume that wherever an author refers to rank, he has also in mind the idea of succession. The Faith and Order document entitled *Baptism, Eucharist and Ministry* contains these passages:

> Clement of Rome linked the mission of the bishop with the sending of Christ by the Father and the sending of the apostles by Christ. This made the bishop a successor of the apostles, ensuring the permanence of the apostolic mission in the Church. . . . Ignatius regards the Christian community assembled around the bishop in the midst of presbyters and deacons as the actual manifestation in the Spirit

of the apostolic community. The sign of apostolic succession thus not only points to historical continuity; it also manifests an actual spiritual reality.[13]

These statements require qualification. Nowhere, from Clement of Rome in the first century to Ignatius in the second to Clement of Alexandria in the third, with all their appetite for rank or their insistence upon office as reaching back to the apostles and thus ordained by God, is there evidence of a theory of apostolic, Petrine succession. In fact, whether or not a bishop worthy of the name even existed in the second-century Antioch of Ignatius is open to dispute. And as for Rome, it first desisted from relying on any fragile chain of successors who might guarantee orthodox teaching.[14] It is true that Clement assumed *order* in the church had existed since apostolic times, and thus may have been the first to derive both order and teaching in the church from the same parent root. But nowhere does Clement describe the bishop as having indelible character, or as irreplaceable, and nowhere does he surrender the Christian congregation's responsibility for itself. And again, though the matter of episcopal monarchy appeared settled for Ignatius—the one bishop embracing the presbyterium and, beneath both, the deacons—nowhere does he lay emphasis on the *apostolic origin* of the order in the congregation, and nowhere does he construe the power of the bishop in legal or juridical fashion. With Ignatius, the old Pauline idea of mutual submission still lives on.

Though Tertullian (as Irenaeus before him) gave classical form to Hegesippus' attempt to trace the office of bishop directly to the apostles, and was even first to give the words in Matthew 16 concerning the "keys" their significance for clerical self-consciousness, neither before nor after his "conversion" to Montanism did he recognize the priesthood as in itself holy or sacral. Early and late, Tertullian regarded the institution of the priesthood as indispensable to the order and dignity of the church, but did not conceive the mediation of salvation as essentially bound to it. The anti-clericalism of Tertullian—first to use the concept of the "universal priesthood of believers"—was not the result of a change in attitude toward the episcopacy as such. Nor was it a struggle for the freedom of the laity for freedom's sake. It was a protest against the "spiritless" tyranny of clerics who used their office to pardon sins which only God would or would not forgive. Not even Cyprian, who abandoned the heroic-enthusiastic radicalism of his master, Tertullian, and with whom the clergy's political self-consciousness became determinative of life in the church, would allow for a succession harking back to Peter, especially not when the Roman bishop laid claim to it. Not till the end of the fourth and the beginning of the fifth century, when politicians had decided the new religion could serve the ends of state, not till the church began in earnest to model itself after imperial government, did that notion of succession emerge. In the beginning, the concept of apostolic succession meant simply the continual fulfillment of the *task of congregational leadership* first assigned by the apostles.[15] The truth of the matter is that the ancient church never made that fatal attempt to exalt the tradition to be taught in the church as from the fathers, and then set it alongside the Scripture as a formal, obligatory canon.[16]

To return to our question: Was this route to order, this preoccupation with rank, with hierarchy and succession resistible? Did the gospel of Paul or the Gnostic threat or the need for visible guarantees in face of Christ's delay—or, better, in face of the hiddenness of an existence determined by the hiddenness of God's conquest in a crucified man—did it create a crisis or necessity sufficient to move the church to take this route? It happened, that is obvious, and whoever supposes that what happens is inevitable has begun an argument I need the help of a philosopher to finish. But it was *resistible.* And it *was* resisted.

The resistance began with a redefinition of power. The gospel was the power, and it was God's. The church did not own it, but had been created by it, and could only serve it. And the character of that power was dialectical—the power of God manifest in the mean figure of a hanged man. If encounter with God occurred in the word about that man, that encounter was not automatic. Mere talk, mere hearing of that man did not guarantee it. Just as that man would have been nothing if God had not made him "power and wisdom," the word about that man was nothing if God did not make something of it. For this reason, speaking or hearing that word could not be identified with God but only with what could be heard or seen. And everything that led up to that speaking or hearing—gifts, capacities, or education, and everything that facilitated that speaking or hearing—structures, institutions, and their occupants, could not be identified with God. It all had to wait for God to make something of it.

Luther's Resistance

If encounter with God occurred in the word about that man, then that word was also a promise, the promise that God would make something of it; that one need not look elsewhere for encounter with God, or despair at being unable to encounter God anywhere at all. But a promise is not a guarantee. Even if there were only a split second between the promise and its fulfillment, the promise, the word, and the service to it would have to wait like a beggar at the door. The power was God's, and everything else a service to it.

The reader will recognize the author behind these words—Martin Luther—although he has often stood as cipher for everything that pronounces benediction on the status quo.

From that redefinition of power, Luther proceeded to distinguish service to it from any other power of rule. It was not that any other power of rule had nothing to do with God. It was not that the power of God in the crucified had nothing to do with any other power of rule. And it was not that these two powers, these "two kingdoms" enjoyed a kind of Zoroastrian coexistence, both here to stay, and to stay as they are. Both were from God, but the one was being squeezed off, overwhelmed, painted into a corner by the other, because the one existed only for the other; because any power of rule other than the power of God in the crucified served the will of God to save. That idea of the "two kingdoms," so often caricatured as a mere distinction between the temporal and spiritual, the one related to the other as body to spirit, belongs to Luther's eschatological vision of the God who was after repossessing everything he had made. Laws and kings were nothing but a hindrance to the hindrance of God's purpose to save. For this reason, shaping the church after the model of any other power than that power of God to save spelled identification with what was passing away. This was one reason why the hierarchical structure was overturned, and Luther would write that a bishop, even the most sainted, had no right to command;[17] that "in the church it is not the succession of the bishops which makes a bishop; the Lord alone is our bishop."[18] This was one reason why he would call any office or institution which pretended to mediate salvation a sign of "Satan's church."[19] As for the pope, he was not in *every* case a false teacher. Just as other bishops he could instruct in evangelical fashion. But by virtue of his office he was the enemy of the freedom of the gospel, in fact, *the* enemy, since he arrogated to himself absolute authority in the church.

There was another reason. And it was *not* that salvation had no link to the present, or to any presently existing thing. It did indeed, though it could not be restricted to the present, as, for example, occurs when justification is reduced to the mere forgiveness of sins. The fellowship with Christ given in justification was a fellowship not only with the One who was or is, but with the One who is to come. So the status of the Christian could not be fixed by any temporal definition. But whatever it was in the present to which salvation was linked was a sign—not the sign of a metaphysical reality transferred to the visible, and requiring guarantee through institutions; and not a sign in the sense of "standing in" for whatever it signified, but a sign as close to what it signified as the flesh of Jesus to the resurrected Christ—the Word heard and seen. And faith would supply the copula, would make what was signified the predicate of the sign—faith, under the category of hope as the access to present and future. But if "by faith," then the church, then life together "in the faith," then structure, order, institution disclosed to faith alone.

Luther knew as well as any that revolution does not proceed according to the rules of conventional warfare, in which men who do not know each other and having nothing against each other kill each other at the command of men who know each other and have everything against each other but do not kill each other (Paul Valery). For this reason, he abandoned whatever earlier notion he may have had of compromise with those people in command.

In his admonition to the clergy at the Diet of Augsburg in 1530, Luther wrote: "Your blood be on your own head! We are and want to be innocent of your blood and damnation."[20] Article 28, §21 of the Augsburg Confession, with its concession to the historic episcopate *de jure divino* (by divine right), is nautical miles from such a declaration.

If service to the power of God, to the world, to the promise that God would make something of it was all, then use was all. Then institution or office stood or fell with whatever use for the other required. Then there was no special power of grace, but only responsibility. Then whatever of legal or juridical form was attached to the office had no intrinsic worth. Then the office of ministry was not an "organ of the church."[21] Then a pastor could "work in the stead of and as the representative of the common assembly and power."[22] Then Christians could desist from their right to preach, teach, and baptize if use was served by transference of that right to a single person. Then ordination or the laying on of hands was similar to the witness of a notary "to a worldly matter."[23] But this did not reduce ordination to a "worldly matter." It was a case of one charism's recognizing another. In ordination, the church attested to its recognition of the ordinand as "gifted" by God and called to the ministerial office. But it was the *church* which attested, not the officeholder, and its action was an *attestation,* nothing more.

Then women could preach. And if Luther added the proviso that they should do so only if men were

absent, since males were better at pulpiteering, that
proviso can hardly be lofted to the status of a dog-
ma.[24] Then the universal priesthood was not an
"organ" of the congregation. Then a bishop could
ordain. Then one could even create an episcopacy,
as Luther did when he consecrated Nicholas Ams-
dorf bishop of Naumburg in 1542 (or Georg von
Anhalt in 1545), for which occasion he penned his
Exempel, einen rechten christlichen Bischof zu weihen.
Then neither hierarchical installation nor democratic choice meant anything, but only an act of
love. But if love was the way the charism should
travel, then use was all, use for the other. And as
for the office itself, the limits set to it were the very
same as were set to all those other powers except
that power of God to save—the limits of time and
space. At the last day "no one would ever preach,"[25]
just as at the last day there would be no kingdoms
of this world but only God "everything to every
one" (1 Cor. 15:28).

Charism, the gift given to all, the criterion of its
genuineness its use for all without thought for rank
or succession—it had all been there in Paul before
his rehabilitation. And it had all been fired by what
Ernst Bloch once called the sole object of human
intent, that to which all human thought does service, the only sphere of thought, the content and
object of speech, scattered in all parts of the world,
hidden in the dark of the moment, promised in the
shape of the absolute question[26]—hope, expectation, hope in God's repossession of the world. None
of the celebrated interpreters of Luther has ever

written about his eschatology. I wonder why. For from this perspective also, the entire theology of the man can be seen. And if Paul could go to such lengths as to lump himself in with the "woes" or "footsteps" of the Messiah as a phenomenon of the "end of days," so could a Luther, as for example in his 1545 preface to Daniel:

> Jan Hus was a forerunner of this time, when he preached to them in the Spirit and said, "you are going to roast a goose [*Hus* means 'goose'], but a swan is coming after me, and you won't roast him." And so it happened. He was burned in the year 1416 [sic]. The present conflict began with indulgences in the year 1517. . . . This is the last time, our time, in which the gospel has filled the place with sound. . . .

There was more behind that utterance then a massive self-consciousness. It was the same conviction as had filled Luther at Worms—that the feverish and unrelenting opposition to the gospel he had preached was the sign of the end. The eschatological view of history which institutional Christianity had abandoned but which had marked earliest Christian faith had been renewed, and at the decisive point: In the experience of God's repossession as shattering the world and the resultant certainty that the end of days was not far off.

Once a revolution takes on concretion, it begins to lose its nimbus. At first the dream shimmers with goodness and purity, and what is not yet reached—

if ever it could be—seems a paradise on earth. But when the dream is realized, it becomes as human a work as anything else—imperfect, as covered with blood and filth as anything else. Lenin's world-revolution ended in Stalin's building a single state, and in between all that carnage, beginning with the murder of Georgians and Lenin's cerebral hemor-rhages. Only two bishops, one from a diocese now in Poland, the other from a diocese near a Soviet park—spots no travel agency ever advertises—only these two attached themselves to the Reformation. As a consequence, princes became protectors of the church. Never mind that their "custody of the two tables," as Melanchthon had called it, assumed that these princes were also confessors, hearers beneath the pulpit. However that notion of custody may have contradicted the tenet of the Peace of Augs-burg of 1555 (*cuius regio, eius religio;* crude transla-tion: "share the religion of your prince or emi-grate!"), what was expedient became permanent. The prince, the ruler was no longer interim-trustee. He had become *summus episcopus,* "highest bishop" of the land. "And so it continued, both day and night" till 1918, till that war "with God for King and Fatherland." Was it resistible, this making a virtue of necessity, and for four hundred years? Was it inevitable, this return to the assumption of direct, immediate access to the "orders of creation," to an understanding of the First Article apart from the Second, and thus this reshaping of the church after the model of empire, and in its wake that man who called himself "the tool of Providence," whose birthdays little boys and girls were told in their primers to celebrate like this:

> The Führer has a birthday. . . . What shall we give him? Our love and our thanks; our whole heart shall be his . . . ?

When Albrecht Dürer heard a rumor of Luther's arrest, he wrote in his diary:

> See how the filthy tyranny of worldly might and the powers of darkness prevail! Hearken, knight of Christ, ride at the Lord's side, defend the truth and grasp the martyr's crown!

To paraphrase a line Humphrey Bogart never spoke in *Casablanca*, "Play it again, Al, play it again!" The power and the charisma and the kingdoms are God's; ours is the use for the other.

4

Where to—Bishop?

The Question of the Nature and Authority of the Episcopal Office

Hiddenness and Visibility

The message of the gospel is that God is repossessing the world; that this conquest began with the cross and resurrection of Jesus Christ, God's Son; that by faith in the Word which heralds that repossession we come to share the life of God. If this is true, then that life which God has given to share has been given to all. Then, in other words, all believers have the Spirit of God, and use, use for the other is the only criterion by which what has been given can be measured as genuine.

There is more to be said of Christian existence than this. What establishes use for the other as sole criterion is the shape of that life we share. The God who in Jesus is winning back the world he made determined that the shape of his conquest would be that which for any other deity spelled an intolerable contradiction, but which for him belonged to the very stuff of Godhead—the shape of the cross. To share the life of this God means to share the shape of that life.

In this connection it is often stated that since the life of God is hidden in the shape it has assumed, the existence of the believer is hidden also. The Paulinist in Colossians writes: "Your life is hid with Christ in God" (Col. 3:3). But by hiddenness he does not mean invisibility. Much of the talk of the visible and invisible church begins with anxiety over visibility, or over a particular understanding of visibility, thus with the attempt to justify Christian existence to the world. That life should assume such shape as that of the One to whom we belong may render existence equivocal and ambiguous, but not invisible. The difference between what we do or attempt and that which anyone else with moral scruple may do or attempt may not be perceptible or measurable, but it is not on that account invisible. The distance between the Gnostic and the pupil of Paul just quoted does not lie in the fact that for the Paulinist life was hidden, whereas for the Gnostic it was not. It lies in the fact that the Christian *still waits* for what the Gnostic believes has already occurred, at least privately to him—a revelation of what is hidden. "We ourselves, who have the first fruits of the Spirit, groan inwardly as we wait for adoption as sons, the redemption of our bodies" (Rom. 8:23). But to share the life of God through faith in the word of his conquest in the cross of his Son does not merely establish Christian existence as dialectical. The God whose life we share is not merely the One who was or is, but also the One who is to come. Resurrection and eternal life belong to justification. But it does mean that till its true identity is made evident, Christian existence is dialectical.

The German Church Struggle and Its Question

The "$64 question" (the phrase is taken from an ancient quiz show, in which the prize never exceeded that modest maximum) is whether or not that shape which our life takes on by virtue of our share in the life of God is limited only to individual, personal, private existence, or is reflected—at least refracted—in how we live with each other, in the structures and institutions we erect to facilitate our life together.

Under their state-appointed bishop, the "German Christians" in June of 1932 laid down the following principle:

> We want the reawakened German sense of vitality respected in our Church. . . . We see in race, folk and nation, orders of existence granted and entrusted to us by God. . . . In the mission to the Jews we perceive a grave danger to our nationality. It is an entrance gate for alien blood into our body politic.

. . . We want an evangelical Church that is rooted in our nationhood.[27]

In response to this structuring of the church after the pattern of Hitler's Führertum, Christians of Lutheran, Reformed, and United Churches, of free synods, church assemblies, and parish organizations, united in the Confessional Synod of the German Evangelical Church at Barmen in July 1933. Among other things, that synod declared:

> The Christian Church is the congregation of the brethren in which Jesus Christ acts presently as the Lord in Word and sacrament through the Holy Spirit. As the Church of pardoned sinners, it has to testify in midst of a sinful world, with its faith as with its obedience, *with its message as with its order,* that it is solely his property, and that it lives and wants to live solely from his comfort and from his direction in the expectation of his appearance.[28]

Once again, a church had structured itself after a state, and this time to a state committed to the extirpation or subjugation of all who were of another race than the Aryan. But the question is whether or not the assertion that the church's structure must conform to its confession stands or falls with the dissolution of Hitler's Reich.

Should the structure of the church conform to the dialectic which characterizes Christian existence? If that dialectic does not occur by accident, or merely because what Christians offer to the world encounters opposition from the world, but by virtue of the shape of that life they share—were it otherwise, Luther wrote, we would be "bastards and not children" of God—should the shape of Christians' life together be determined by historical accident or by whatever exists outside it? Should it be any less a reflection that they are not bastards but children? If baptism is rendered harmless by setting the community which it establishes into invisibility, or when the heaven in that "forum" of which justification takes place becomes pagan—a distant, indeterminate place, separated from the word of God's conquest in the here and now—is it rendered any the less harmless by structures which contradict the shape of the life which baptism sets in motion, by institutions which attempt to overleap the dialectic in an anticipation of what is still to come?

The German church struggle gave to these questions more than academic significance. It lifted them from the context of the *adiaphoron*, of what is indifferent, to the level of a test of faith. Not every Lutheran embraced the Barmen Declaration—not even every Lutheran who participated in its discussion. But when the Prussian church applied the "Aryan paragraph" of the law of 1933, excluding Jews from office in the state to Jews holding office in the church—and on its own initiative, without any pressure from the state—at least one Lutheran dissenter wrote that its adoption was "a blasphemy against the Holy Spirit for which there is no forgiveness, neither in this world nor in the next."[29]

Lutheran Advocacy of the Episcopate

Where to—bishop? In the Roman Catholic church, the episcopal structure is regarded as fixed by divine decree (*jure divino*). However broad the current interpretation of that tenet, it still means that only a bishop may ordain, since only the bishop is the recipient of that specific and discrete grace for oversight harking back to Christ and the apostles. Prior to the Reformation, a few held that a priest could ordain, but only on condition he had been authorized to do so by the pope. Thus, in 1400, Pope Boniface IX authorized an English abbot to conduct the consecration of his priests.

For centuries, the Anglican Church has laid claim to apostolic, Petrine succession, a claim which Rome did not contest till 1896, and which, in light of the altered historical and theological situation, Rome may once again allow. Thus, when German Lutheran and Evangelical pastors, driven out by Hitler, requested that the Bishop of Chicester allow them into his diocese, he required not merely that they be reordained but also undergo confirmation instruction.

In Rome and at Canterbury, the view is fixed that any office or structure other than the episcopal designed to implement the heralding of God's redemptive activity is "defective." In agreement with this tenet, the document entitled *Facing Unity*, and to which both Catholics and Lutherans are signatories, encourages a remedying of the defect through an "initial act of recognition" of ministry on both sides, leading to a single episcopate of Catholic and Lutheran churches in collegial form, and culminating in a common ordained ministry. Would this not mean an ordination to ministry at the hands of bishops who enjoy apostolic succession?[30]

Lutheran interest in the establishment of the episcopal office is not new. Agitation for supervision of the church through some type of episcopal office is a part of our own history, studded with the names of Theodor Kliefoth of Mecklenburg (1810–1895); Wilhelm Löhe of Neuendettelsau (1808–1872); the Jewish convert Friedrich Julius Stahl (1802–1861), and August Vilmar of Marburg (1800–1868). Convinced that the doctrine of salvation had reached the zenith of its expression, they contended that a doctrine of the church as an objective institution for salvation needed developing.

In the library of my school, I stumbled across a pamphlet written 90 years ago by a member of the Iowa ministerium, and entitled: "The Episcopal Form of Government Is the Only Legitimate Form for the Church in General and the Only Adequate Form for the Lutheran Church in Particular." It ends with these words:

> The famous pastor Loehe, who should have been a bishop according to the grace which God had given him, and who as bishop would have wrought still more blessed works than he did, once said, that the Lutheran Church should really present itself as an Episcopal Church of Brethren. I, too, close this paper with the words: "Ceterum censeo, episcopatum

pro ecclesia nostra esse restituendum" ("be it further resolved that for the sake of our Church the
episcopacy be restored").[31]

Current Lutheran arguments for establishing the
episcopal office are many and varied. One is that
the episcopacy will remove previously existing barriers to fellowship among Christians; that it will
promote a greater visible unity of the church
through the oneness of its public ministry. For this
reason it has been argued that ordination as a sign
of apostolic succession through the episcopal laying
on of hands is to be greeted, and where it is lacking,
to be striven for.

The statement entitled "Lutheran Understanding
of the Episcopal Office," produced by The Lutheran
World Federation Department of Studies, reads, in
part, that persons in episcopal ministries are called
to exercise leadership in the church by "expressing
and serving the unity of the Church in relating to
other churches and to confessional and ecumenical
organizations."[32] The statement has its echo in the
Consensus of the Consultation on Church Union, according to which the bishops have an obligation

> to call the churches to the goal of visible unity in
> one faith and one eucharistic fellowship expressed
> in worship and in common life in Christ, and to
> advance toward that unity that the world may be-
> lieve.[33]

Another argument is that the episcopate is necessary because "it alone can guarantee authority of

administration and spiritual care." The words are Julius Stahl's, but the argument is still fresh. One contemporary writes that in the presence of the congregation the pastor is teacher of the gospel; that no superior body can free the pastor of this responsibility, but then asks: "Who is the teacher of the clergy?" In answer, the author states that the work of theological faculties obviously cannot exercise the churchly office of teaching, but have merely the function of serving that office. The writer concludes that only a bishop can exercise such an office, and which he describes as by "divine right."[34]

Another argument reads that the establishment of the episcopate in the Lutheran church will result in parity with the Roman Catholic church, and still another that it would serve to represent the church in the public sector.[35]

The Appeals

All these arguments are in some measure reinforced by appeals to the Reformers and the Lutheran Confessions. For example, the document *Facing Unity* states that

The Lutheran Reformation basically affirmed the episcopal office of the Early Church. There was readiness to retain the episcopal office in its traditional form, even though there was criticism of the manner in which the office was exercised at that time.[36]

And in fact, §21 of the German and Latin editions of Article 28 of the Augsburg Confession does refer to the bishop's "divine right" to

> preach the Gospel, forgive sins, judge doctrine and condemn doctrine that is contrary to the Gospel, and exclude from the Christian community the ungodly whose wicked conduct is manifest.[37]

Appeal is also made to Philip Melanchthon's suggestion of an "evangelical papacy," as contained in his addition to the signature of the Smalcald Articles. The addition reads:

> Concerning the pope I hold that, if he would allow the Gospel we, too, may concede to him that superiority over the bishops which he possesses by human right, making this concession for the sake of peace and general unity among the Christians who are now under him and who may be in the future.[38]

And, in a letter to a friend at Nürnberg, Melanchthon wrote:

> Oh, that I were able to restore the administration of bishops. For I see what sort of Church we are about to have—a lax [the term used was *dissoluta*] ecclesiastical polity. I see coming a far more intolerable future tyranny than ever existed before.[39]

Finally, when *Facing Unity* describes the interval between the reciprocal recognition of ministries by

Catholics and Lutherans, and the ultimate goal of a common ordained ministry under a single *episcopē* or supervision as "a period of transition vouchsafed by God,"[40] the inference to be drawn is that the establishment of the episcopacy is by divine sanction; that the bishopric is God's will.

Appeal to the Confessions is fairly universal among Lutherans, though between parties of opposing sentiments it usually results in a tie, since almost all agree that the Confessions are not calculated to facilitate detour around decisions which the church must make respecting its life. But it is true that in light of the discussions which preceded the drafting of Article 28 in the Augsburg Confession, what is written there respecting the episcopate is much less an advocacy than a concession; further, a concession which had not been anticipated prior to its framing.[41] (Actually, if Luther had not fixed the principles for interpreting those articles "about matters in dispute," among them Article 28; if he had not stiffened Melanchthon's hand, what appears merely as a concession would have been an outright compromise.) To cite but one example from this period, Luther's sermon "That One Should Keep Children at School," completed in July 1530, makes clear how far the Reformer had removed himself from the historic episcopacy.

As for Melanchthon, while it is true that between him and Luther the rejection of the historic episcopate always remained open, he nevertheless did describe it as by "human" authority, not "divine right." In fact, he wrote of the episcopal office as "added" for utilitarian reasons.[42] And because Melanchthon regarded what existed by "human right" as alterable (clearly reflected in the context of the Augsburg Confession, Article 28), his private opinion respecting the church's structure—an opinion determined by concern for pedagogy and not for cultic form, though resting on a metaphysical argument to which his friend would not consent—cannot be construed as valid for all time.[43] As for the implication that the historic episcopate is willed by God—that is a move from the citing of a mere concession or a private opinion which I am unable to make.

Episcopacy and the Office of Ministry as Sacrament

Where to—bishop? Perhaps in the train of Melanchthon, Stahl, and others who urged it for purposes of discipline ("Who is the teacher of the clergy?"), a few advocates of episcopacy in the Lutheran church detach from it any sacramental character, construing the office exclusively in terms of function. According to this view, the only difference between the episcopal office and that of the pastor of a congregation consists in the bishop's supervision within a larger area. The distinction between bishop and pastor is thus identical or similar to that between pastor and laity as conceived, for example, by the Constitution of The American Lutheran Church. The relevant sentences read:

> Individuals, clergy and lay, belong to The American
> Lutheran Church by virtue of their membership in

one of its constituent congregations. The status of the clergy differs from that of the laity only as to function.[44]

This functional view is what appears to underlie the appropriation of the episcopal title among former district presidents of The American Lutheran Church, though few would admit to exercising any pedagogical function. On occasion, one or two have complained that they are merely ecclesiastical social workers without privilege.

On the other side, the majority of the advocates of episcopacy attach sacramental significance to the office. Their defense usually begins with the description of ordination to public ministry as a sacrament. In one argument, the ascension of Christ, his coming into kingly rule, is described as temporally and signally visible and effective in the act of ordination.[45] In another, the act of ordination by the laying on of hands is described as at one and the same time invocation of the Holy Spirit, a sacramental sign, and an acknowledgment of gifts and commitment.[46] In still another, ordination is described as a gift of grace of the Holy Spirit for lifetime ministry.[47] At this point, reference may be made to the "polarity" of the sacramental, that is, to the sacrament's embracing tradition and kerygma or *signum* and *res*, the sign and what is signified, a polarity to which it is said the structure of the church must correspond. In ordination, this correspondence is reflected in the polarity of the pastoral office and the congregation. And since at ordination the polarity of the individual congregation and the entire church requires expression, it falls to the bishop in whom both these polarities intersect, to perform the act of ordination. He alone can give to ordination the character it requires as sacramental sign. Indifference toward the expression of this polarity, it is argued, spells a denial of the character of the sacramental sign as well as of the structure of the church.[48]

This description of the episcopal office as guaranteeing sacramental character to ordination is at times accompanied by reference to the title allegedly held by priests in ancient Israel who were responsible for the examination of the purity of animals for sacrifice, a title assumed by leaders of the Qumran community. Aside from the fact that no fixed definition can be assigned the Hebrew or Septuagint counterparts to our term *bishop,* or from the fact that the office of supervision (*episkepsis*) at Qumran was restricted to the moral or religious purity of the sect (a concept echoed, for example, in Rom. 15:15-16), the reference is calculated to link the office of bishop with the liturgical or cultic.

Concomitant with the advocacy of episcopacy is the emphasis on the Lord's Supper as a "Eucharist," as "an act of thanksgiving," described by the Lutheran *Manual on the Liturgy* as "the Christians' principal act of worship."[49] Whether or not the concomitance spells return to the ancient notion of ordination as granting the Spirit for the purpose of repeating the sacrifice of Christ in the Mass is surely open to doubt. But that the linking of the two interests is nothing more than coincidence is surely

open to question. The connection of episcopacy
with priestly service, and the language currently
used of the Lord's Supper is an obvious nod in the
direction of the cultic or sacrificial. But what was it
that occurred on the cross? Or what occurs in sacramental proclamation of the Lord's death "until he
comes"? The cross was certainly not a "satisfaction"
or an act to be construed in terms of cause and
effect—the death the cause and the sinner's justification its effect. Luther had an aversion to the
transference into theology of concepts from the natural sciences. It was scholastic theology which
emerged from such transference, and from which
he advised his readers to exert all their energy to
get free. "But if you ever choose to use such terms,"
he said, "then please give them a thorough scrub-
bing beforehand; take them to the tub."[50] Anyone
with a modicum of acquaintance with current phil-
osophical discussion will find echoes to that aversion. The "arts," the humane sciences (and that includes theology), cannot be described in terms of
the concepts of the natural sciences. The subject
matter of the "arts" does not lie flat, but encounters
us through a multiplicity of voices from the past
and filling our historical consciousness. And for the
"arts," everything hangs on that encounter. In any
case, what occurs in the sacrament cannot be the
representation or repetition of what the death on
the cross never was.

Where to—bishop? The question concerning the
establishment of the episcopacy is only part of the
larger question as to whether or not whatever

Christians construct for their common life together shall conform to their confession. But the current preoccupation with the episcopal office brings that larger question into sharper focus.

Return to the Arguments for the Episcopate

We turn once more to the arguments in favor of episcopacy. First, it is stated that it will demonstrate the church's visible unity through the oneness of its ministry; second, that it will guarantee authority to administration and spiritual care; third, that it will furnish parity with Rome, and fourth, that it will facilitate representation of the church to the public sector. And at the base, or perhaps at the apex—at any rate in the company of these arguments—there is a conception of the episcopal office as furnishing ordination with sacramental character, the character that it is said ordination requires. Visible unity, then, for the sake of the church's own self-consciousness; the guarantee of authority for the sake of disciplining the "faithful"; equality for the sake of amity or reciprocity between the two great contenders within the church throughout 400 years of its history, and visible unity again, this time for the sake of representation to the world.

Can these things be achieved, and can they be achieved through the episcopal office? The answer is that they can be achieved because they *have already* been achieved—from the end of the 4th to the end of the 16th centuries. Agreed, the first and the last phases of that achievement were its worst. It began with the imposition of Christianity by force and ended with the harassment and obliteration of Jews, Muslims, and Christians of opposing sects. But if human beings are more durable than the structures they erect, the evils attending that 1300-year achievement need not be repeated. Our wheels are not different in kind from those wooden discs someone thought to invent before thinking to invent history. But they are cast from molds, have hubs, are attached with bolts and cushioned with rubber.

Some regard the struggle for such an achievement as a mere attempt to turn back the clock. They point to episcopacy as the concomitant, if not the offspring of types of society which the human race has learned to throw off, or whose reappearance in the modern era is regarded as aberrant. They describe this urge for episcopacy as an attempt to return to monarchy, perhaps even to patriarchy. And is it accidental, for example, that in the document which serves as basis for the present discussion between Lutherans and Catholics, the bishop who was and is and is yet to be is continuously referred to in the masculine?

> The bishop is a baptized member of the local koinonia. In the ordination, *he,* as one who is baptized, receives the call of the church. . . . The action of the Holy Spirit . . . is not intended for *his own* well-being . . . but . . . places *him* in its service. . . . When the candidate answers the ordination questions and confesses *his* faith . . . the congregation is witness

that the bishop represents the authentic apostolic faith. . . . As leader of *his own* church together with the other bishops . . . *he* is to bear witness to the faith received from the apostles and watch over it.[51]

Others regard the struggle as leading inevitably to the torpor and passivity inherent in a single state or institution. David Hume and Edward Gibbon sang the praises of the dynamism of the 18th-century Western world with its fractured structure, contrasting it with the sluggishness of united, imperial Rome. Hume wrote that the mutual jealousy of neighboring states

keeps them from receiving too lightly the law from each other, in matters of taste and of reasoning, and makes them examine every work of art with the greatest care and accuracy. The contagion of popular opinion spreads not so easily from one place to another. It readily receives a check in some state or other.[52]

This argument has had its echo in the church. In an address delivered to pastors 43 years ago by the president of a theological seminary now merged with my own, he gave definition to the idea which served as the rationale for the synod to which he belonged. In it he stated that the Lutheran Free Church had consistently stressed the principle of congregational independence, a principle by no means unique to it, but with special implication for it, since bound up with a "revolt against too strong synodical domination." He referred to the founders of his denomination who were convinced that the advantages gained by a strong central organization in the church were more than outweighed by the disadvantages and evils of concentrated authority, and concluded that if emphasis upon spiritual awakening and congregational freedom and responsibility should be sacrificed upon the altars of ecclesiastical uniformity and doctrinal rigor, the whole Lutheran household of faith would be the poorer for it.[53]

Church Structure and the Dialectic of Christian Existence

These criticisms have validity, but the conditions against which they are directed may mirror something deeper: an eagerness to compensate for the dialectic of Christian existence; to exchange that dialectic for what could justify such existence—to oneself and to the world. Or, if the dialectic is ineradicable, the conditions may mirror an eagerness to arrange some justification for the dialectic itself— something analogous to the notion that the perception in oneself of the tension between good and evil is proof of the presence of faith.

How to match that urge for visibility, for guarantees, for parity, for representation with the word that God makes conquest in the world in the cruciform shape of those who are his? How to square acknowledgment of that dialectic with structures erected to resolve it? Or, how to reconcile the idea of ordination as guaranteeing sacramental character through the visible imposition of hands by persons laying claim to visible, episcopal succession with those acts whose visibility defies guarantees, and precisely because they are the signs of the humanity of the One who repossesses the world in such contrary and paradoxical fashion, a visibility which requires belief, belief that the One who promises to encounter us in such mean things will keep that promise—Baptism and the Supper? How does such a concept reflect that gulf between visibility and guarantees which marks the sovereignty of the God who will be encountered only where the audible or the visible can be opposed, pilloried, crucified, or believed?

We are on the eve of a gigantic ecclesiastical amalgamation. To some it may appear to refract merely that typical American obsession with quantity. Consider, for a moment, the structure of the state, merely with reference to foreign policy. The president has a National Security Council, embracing a smaller staff of some 400 people—the size of a parliament—and a larger, embracing some 3000—the size of any European assembly. The CIA, the Office of Information, of Agriculture, of Welfare, the diverse private and semiprivate organizations, to say nothing of Congress—each has its foreign-political program and mandate. And whoever imagines that that mightiest state within the state—the Pentagon—represents a single, integrated unit, is mistaken. Each of its branches—the Army, the Marines, and the Air Force—has its own section devoted to affairs overseas. Wags in Washington predict World War III will break out between the Army and the Air Force. American foreign policy appears to be the result of a struggle within its own bureaucracy.

By virtue of mass alone, the new Evangelical Lutheran Church in America will be visible enough. But the question is whether or not to give to that visibility the same character as attaches to Christian existence; whether or not the structure of the new body can in any way be made conformable to its confession.

And what occurs when that urge for visibility with guarantees, for a visibility which is undialectic, unambiguous, is matched against the Word of God's conquest? If one were to reply, "the Word loses; the Word takes second seat," he or she would be wrong. The Word does not lose, no matter how many bitter things occur with the attempt to humble it—restriction of the common priesthood to mere private or public prayer or to the mere ratification of decisions already made by superiors; return of the female to the pew in exchange for apostolic succession; the apathy of the world toward the visible, the image, the symbol, once it has seen it a hundred times. The Word does not lose, because it belongs to the God who is repossessing the world. The church loses, the church with all its horror of the dialectic, of the meanness of the revelation which creates it; the church is shattered and trampled by what that meanness hides. This is why advocacy of monarchical or patriarchal succession for the purpose of guaranteeing the office of the ministry is irrelevant. This is why the advocacy of democratic transference for the purpose of guaranteeing the right of the universal priesthood is irrelevant. This is why all discussion of imbalance between the two as symptom of the crisis in ministry or as the crisis itself—why all talk of achieving balance between them as alleviating the symptom or the crisis—is irrelevant. It is irrelevant because it assumes that the Word requires deciding for or against its conquest, when in reality the only decision left to the church is whether or not it will submit to the conquest and shape its existence to it, or be overtaken by it, trampled by it, and for one more time! The Word makes its way, and as ineluctably as destiny.

God has established the Word which has created the church which calls to the service of the Word. This is a primitive thing. But this may be as good a time as any to utter such primitive things, since it appears we are being thrust toward them once more, and called to preserve ourselves in them once more. The crisis in ministry is not a lack of balance, but that *none rules*, none but the One who bends present to future, for whom status, rank, title by transmission or by transference are nothing beside his name, his kingdom, and his will. The crisis is that with this God the only measure of the integrity of a gift is its use. The crisis of the ministerial office is that the clergy does not expect that the study of theology in preparation for public service to that Word is nothing but technical preparation for that shape which the One who makes conquest in the world takes in *all* who embrace it—indifference, resistance, exhaustion, increase in mortality rate, domestic shipwreck—a preparation for use, since use is all. The crisis arises from an alteration of faith, from aversion to the dialectic, the hiddenness, the meanness of the visible sign, and the substitution of a visibility which carries the warranty of a shorter gap, a tinier interval between promise and fulfillment. The crisis in ministry is the exchange of the eschatological for the myth of the church; of the application to the church of what can only be said of God; of the church as an extension of deity; of the church's gradual and continuous penetration of the world, and for the sake of this myth harking back to structures and orders in a world to which Christ had not yet come, to ideas and notions underlying those structures to which Christ was still unknown.

In closing, a few words from someone who no doubt stated it better than I could:

Where . . . God's lordship in this time cannot be separated from the crucified Christ, all churches and believers are at best signs and instruments of the end-time broken in, of that fulfillment in which God alone will rule the world, his rivals and enemies destroyed. Of this end they should surely be signs and instruments, if God himself is not to be blasphemed as unworthy of belief. Viewed from such a task, the pluriformity without which there has never been a Christian ecumene assumes positive aspect: When God comes to us, none goes away empty, none may be exempt from service. Each owes the common Lord a witness. . . . In the New Testament there was not yet what we call "laity," only the priestly members of the people of God. The Spirit of the present Christ requires the infinite number and variety of the functions of his earthly body, in order to reach to every place on the globe. . . . God does not create uniformity. His kingdom works the solidarity of the unlike, because Christ died for all and can use each in his service.[54]

Afterword

The Reformation understanding of the gospel is distinguished by its attitude toward the "sign"—the Word of God preached or made visible in the sacrament, and "what is signified"—encounter with God, "forgiveness of sins, life and salvation." On the one hand, that understanding refuses to identify the "sign" or Word of God as guarantee of encounter with God. Faith, belief is linked to the Word as *promise.* While the Word itself announces that God will keep his promise and encounter us in that Word, at the same time it announces that God is sovereign over that encounter. In other words, the Word itself declares that it is promise, not guarantee. On the other hand, the Reformation understanding rejects the notion of "sign" as something which "stands in" for or "represents" what it signifies, as though another, third entity were interposed between the Word of God and encounter with God. Faith, belief is linked to the Word as promise, but it is precisely *to this Word* that it is linked.

The implications for ministry contained in this dialectic are twofold. First, no structure or organization can be established which would alter the character of the Word of God as promise to the Word of God as guarantee. No authority in the church can screen the character of faith as trust in the Word as the promise of God. Second, no structure or organization can be established which would alter the character of the Word from being "secular" or "this-worldly" to the Word as sacral or "other-worldly." No authority in the church can screen the character of the Word of God made audible or visible through human speech and action.

This dialectic and its implications have relevance for the question of church structure—specifically, for the question of the shape of ministry. During the discussions following the lectures, I was frequently asked to relate my argument to the problem of the precise form which the new Evangelical Lutheran Church in America should take. While the attempt to answer that question would have strained the limits of my competence, the question is not irrelevant. But the question deserves second place. Until an answer is given to the question, Shall the structure of the church conform to its confession? or, Shall the form of those churches which call themselves after the Reformation conform to the dialectic of encounter with God in a this-worldly Word? the question of shape is rash, precipitate. It was that prior question of conformity that I meant to address, and which falls within the area of my responsibility as student of Scripture. In the ancient church, that question of conformity of structure with confession was, if not always explicitly, then surely more implicitly put than many have been ready to admit.

If structure or order, if the shape of ministry deserves only second seat, it does, for all that, still deserve a seat, and once it is clear from whence it derives its right of place, the question concerning the nature of that place takes on significance. Rudolf Bultmann once wrote that the discussion between Rudolf Sohm and Adolf von Harnack had not yet been concluded.[55] With respect to the actual situation prevailing in the Protestant sector, that judgment may be true. But the record of the New Testament, the inferences to be drawn from the history of the ancient church, and the attitude of the Reformers—Luther in particular—indicate that what prevails is not inevitable. It is not inevitable that the church should live from the continuity or solidarity of its structure. Nor is it inevitable that the church should live from the discontinuity and arbitrariness of eternal reform. It was and still is possible for the church to embrace an order which does not take on a separate or even salutary significance which cancels out trust alone in the Word of God as promise. And since that promise is for all, it was and still is possible for the church's order to be "exoteric" in nature, that is, structured for the sake of (not according to the pattern of) the world. For this reason, the church may even battle for order against stubborn and willful individualism, but always in the consciousness that the redemption of the other may require alteration or replacement in structure. "Use is all!" In other words, ministry, order, structure, is a work of love. This is precisely what is meant by the characterization of the Word as "secular," "this-worldly," and this is the principle which the Reformation regained, and by which order was neither rejected nor deified.

With respect to the episcopal office, it is no secret that for Luther neither the removal of visible barriers between Christians nor guaranteeing the authority of administration nor ecumenicity yielded sufficient reason for its existence. "Visitation" should comprise its heart and soul. If the episcopacy should exist at all, then for the sake of attending to the proper proclamation of the Word as promise to the world that in Jesus Christ God is winning back what he had made. When it was suggested during the discussions that my critique of the episcopal office was tailored exclusively to the Roman model, I replied that in my judgment the bulk of literature on the subject to which Lutherans and Catholics were signatories adhered to that model; that for this reason I felt no obligation to critique or to advocate models in other communions. And in that literature I found nothing which gave to "visitation" the lion's share.

In this country, Lutheranism has been attracted by notions of the "sign" as guarantee (the most telltale symptom of which may be the still regnant dispute over "verbal inspiration"), or by the "sign" as standing in for a reality which it can only mirror, and has structured itself accordingly. The reason often given is that the Lutheran church lacks a "doctrine of the ministry." The statement is obscure, if not downright false. For the Reformers, "ministry" should assume its shape in conformity with the understanding of the Word of God as promise, and of faith as linked to the promise without requiring guarantees. In other words, where the "gift" or "office" of ministry was at issue, first priority was given to that toward which the gift or office should be bent. Preachers and hearers constituted the primal office of the church—preachers responsible for hearers, and hearers responsible for preachers.

In the earlier decades of this century, scholars suggested that the Lutheran church in this country had a toehold on the future. It did so, not merely because its late appearance on the scene held it aloof from disputes which had long since taken on rigidity in other Protestant bodies, but because its link with the "tradition" had equipped it with the capacity for inquiry. But where that link is struck, there is little inquiry, only ideology. Whether or not Lutheranism in this country is desirous of putting the question of conformity between what it confesses and what it constructs for Christians' life together, and as a possible result, of existing as "alien" in a society for the sake of which it nevertheless exists—wherever that prior question of conformity is put, a "Lutheran" understanding of order, of ministry will persist. The persistence of a

Lutheran understanding within a denomination which calls itself Lutheran may be quite another matter. Therein consists the crisis—things may go either way.

Notes

1. *Lutheran Book of Worship* (Minneapolis: Augsburg, and Philadelphia: Board of Publication, Lutheran Church in America, 1978), p. 56.
2. Ernst Fincke, "Das Amt der Einheit," in *Das Amt der Einheit,* essays by Wilhelm Stählin, Johann Heinrich Lerche, Ernst Fincke, Laurentius Klein, and Karl Rahner (Stuttgart: Schwabenverlag, 1964), p. 154.
3. *Occasional Services: A Companion to Lutheran Book of Worship* (Minneapolis: Augsburg, and Philadelphia: Board of Publication, Lutheran Church in America), p. 196.
4. Ernst Käsemann, "Ministry and Community in the New Testament," in *Essays on New Testament Themes,* trans. W. J. Montague (London: SCM, 1964), p. 75.
5. Rudolf Sohm, *Wesen und Ursprung des Katholizismus* (Leipzig: B. G. Teubner, 1909), p. 390.
6. My translation; Adolf Harnack, "Kritik der Abhandlung Rudolf Sohm's *Wesen und Ursprung des Katholizismus,"* in *Entstehung und Entwickelung der Kirchenverfassung und des Kirchenrechts in den zwei ersten Jahrhunderten* (Leipzig: J. C. Hinrichs'sche Buchhandlung, 1910), pp. 174 and 157; cf. Adolf Harnack, *The Constitution and Law of the Church in the First Two Centuries,* trans. F. L. Pogson (London: Williams and Norgate, 1910), pp. 244 and 222.
7. Käsemann, "Ministry and Community in the New Testament," p. 93.
8. Sebastian Haffner, *Zur Zeitgeschichte* (Munich: Theodor Knaur Nachfolger, 1982), p. 216.

9. *Trimorphic Protennoia* 13, 1, 44:15, in *The Nag Hammadi Library in English,* trans. James M. Robinson et al. (New York: Harper and Row, 1977), p. 467.

10. First Clement 54:2, in *The Apostolic Fathers,* trans. Kirsopp Lake, The Loeb Classical Library (Cambridge, Mass.: Harvard University Press, 1970), 1:101.

11. Ignatius, *Phil.* 7:1, *The Apostolic Fathers,* 1:244f.

12. *The Stromata (Miscellanies)* 2.29; 6.18; 7.9, *The Ante-Nicene Fathers,* trans. Alexander Roberts and James Donaldson (New York: Scribners, 1903), 2:369, 520, 538.

13. *Baptism, Eucharist and Ministry,* Faith and Order Paper No. 111 (Geneva: World Council of Churches, 1982), p. 29.

14. Walter Bauer, *Orthodoxy and Heresy in Earliest Christianity,* translated by a team from the Philadelphia Seminar on Christian Origins (Philadelphia: Fortress, 1971), pp. 64 and 120.

15. For the brief survey above, I am indebted to the studies of Hans Freiherr von Campenhausen, *Ecclesiastical Authority and Spiritual Power in the Church of the First Three Centuries,* trans. J. A. Baker (Stanford: Stanford University Press, 1969), pp. 90-94, 96-102, 265-292. Due to the incompleteness of the historical record, the dispute with von Campenhausen's work, at least till now, has been confined to the inferences which he draws respecting the attitudes toward "gift" and "office" in the Christianity of the second and third centuries. But anyone can dispute inferences. In my judgment, von Campenhausen's refusal to embrace Sohm's theory of an unreconcilable contrast between "church" and "church law," or his refusal to embrace von Harnack's sociological explanation for the rise of hierarchy, does justice to the

witness of the New Testament and the postapostolic periods. Both rejected positions lack historical foundation.

16. Cf. von Campenhausen, "Das Problem der Ordnung im Urchristentum und in der alten Kirche," in *Bindung und Freiheit in der Ordnung der Kirche* (Tübingen: J. C. B. Mohr, 1959), p. 19.

17. "Quod ne sanctus Episcopus ius habeat dominandi . . . at illi sunt haeretici, volunt in destructionem dominari," *De Potestate Leges Ferendo in Ecclesia*, 1530 (W.A. 30, 2, 681ff.).

18. Quoted in Heinrich Vogel, *Wer Regiert die Kirche?* Theologische Existenz Heute 15 (1934), p. 18.

19. "Dicimus autem nos Ipsos esse Synagogam Sathanae, non Ecclesiam" *De Potestate*, 685f.

20. "Exhortation to All Clergy Assembled at Augsburg," *Luther's Works*, American Edition, vol. 34 (Philadelphia: Fortress, 1960), p. 60; cf. pp. 44-45: "Christendom has been sustained for many hundreds of years without such endowment bishops and canons and it can well be maintained without them in the future. At the last judgment, certainly no Christian soul will be able to boast or testify that in so many hundreds of years anyone ever heard or learned from his endowment bishop the Lord's Prayer, Ten Commandments, the Creed, or a Gospel or ever felt or benefited by a single episcopal duty or work."

21. Cf. F. J. Stahl, *Die Kirchenverfassung nach Lehre und Recht der Protestanten* (Erlangen: Theodor Bläsing, 1840), pp. 68ff.; T. F. D. Kliefoth, *Liturgische Abhandlungen* (Schwerin: Stiller'schen Hof-Buchhandlung, 1854), 1:351ff.

22. "Dr. Luther's Retraction of the Error Forced upon him by the Most Highly Learned Priest of God, Sir Jerome

Emser, Vicar in Meissen," *Luther's Works,* American Edition, vol. 39 (Philadelphia: Fortress, 1970), p. 237.

23. "Aufflegunge der Hende, die Segenen, bestattigen und bezeugen solchs, wie ein Notarius und zeugen eine Weltliche sache bezeugen," *Exempel, einen rechten christlichen Bischof zu weihen, Geschehen zu Naumburg Anno 1542, 20. Januar* (W.A. 53, 257, 7).

24. "The Misuse of the Mass," *Luther's Works,* American Edition, vol. 36 (Philadelphia: Fortress, 1959), pp. 151-152.

25. "Wirt man nymmer predigen noch glewben, da wirt yderman sehen und fulen," *Die Epistell tzu der Mess ynn der Christnacht,* 1522 (W.A. 10, l, 1, 44, 14).

26. Ernst Bloch, *Religion im Erbe* (Munich: Siebenstern Taschenbuch Verlag, 1966), p. 36.

27. Quoted in Arthur C. Cochrane, *The Church's Confession under Hitler* (Philadelphia: Westminster, 1962), pp. 222-223.

28. In Cochrane, *The Church's Confession,* p. 240; emphasis added.

29. Letter of Herman Sasse to Dietrich Bonhoeffer, in Bonhoeffer, *Gesammelte Schriften,* ed. Eberhard Bethge (Munich: Christian Kaiser Verlag, 1959), 2:71.

30. *Facing Unity, Models, Forms and Phases of Catholic–Lutheran Church Fellowship* (Geneva: Lutheran World Federation, 1985), pp. 57-62.

31. A paper read by Ferdinand Julius G. Stuermer before the Lutheran Convention for the Study of Church Polity (Philadelphia: Excelsior Printing Co., 1896), p. 7.

32. Department of Studies, The Lutheran World Federation, Geneva, 1983, p. 11.

33. *The COCU Consensus: In Quest of a Church of Christ Uniting,* ed. Gerald F. Moede (Baltimore, 1984), p.

50, citing the Constitution of the World Council of Churches.

34. Johann Heinrich Lerche, "Das Bischofsamt in der Evangelisch-Lutherischen Kirche," in *Das Amt der Einheit*, pp. 71-73.
35. "Lutheran Understanding of the Episcopal Office," p. 11.
36. *Facing Unity*, p. 49.
37. In *The Book of Concord*, trans. and ed. Theodore B. Tappert (Philadelphia: Fortress, 1959), p. 84.
38. Smalcald Articles, in *The Book of Concord*, pp. 316-317.
39. Quoted in Stuermer, p. 5.
40. *Facing Unity*, p. 62.
41. Wilhelm Maurer, *Historical Commentary on the Augsburg Confession*, trans. H. George Anderson (Philadelphia: Fortress, 1986), pp. 65-67.
42. *Corpus Reformatorum*, ed. C. G. Bretschneider (Halis Saxonum: C. A. Schwetschke et Filium, 1837), 4:368.
43. Cf. Maurer, *Historical Commentary*, pp. 75, 77.
44. *The Constitution and Bylaws of The American Lutheran Church*, edition of 1987, §§6.32-33, p. 59.
45. Cf. Fincke, "Das Amt der Einheit," p. 113.
46. *Baptism, Eucharist and Ministry*, p. 30.
47. *Facing Unity*, pp. 33, 49, 61.
48. Fincke, "Das Amt der Einheit," pp. 160-161.
49. *Manual on the Liturgy—Lutheran Book of Worship* (Minneapolis: Augsburg, 1979), p. 199.
50. "Si tamen vultis uti vocabulis istis, prius quaeso illa bene purgate, füret sie mal zum Bade," *Die Promotionsdisputation von Palladius und Tilemann*, 1. Juni 1537 (W.A. 39, 1, 229, 6).
51. *Facing Unity*, pp. 50-51.

52. "Of the Rise and Progress of the Arts and Sciences," in David Hume, *Essays Moral, Political and Literary* (London: Oxford University Press, 1963), p. 121.
53. "The Idea of the Lutheran Free Church," in *Freedom and Christian Education,* ed. John A. Houkom (1945), pp. 33-46.
54. Ernst Käsemann, "Die endzeitliche Königsherrschaft Gottes," in *Kirchliche Konflikte* (Göttingen: Vandenhoeck und Ruprecht, 1982), 1:223.
55. Rudolf Bultmann, *Theology of the New Testament,* trans. Kendrick Grobel (New York: Scribners, 1955), 2:95.